TIMBER!

written by
Mary A Livingston

illustrated by
Tim Livingston

RedTail Publishing
Anderson, CA, U.S.A.

Tat-a-tat-pat. Tat-a-tat-pat. Woodpeckers gobble up fetal beetle bugs. The overgrown forest is abuzz with activity.

A wildlife biologist tunes her radio. *Whirrrrrr-irrrrrr-boop-boop-boop.* She spots a fisher dashing over a log. She counts all critters in burrows and trees.

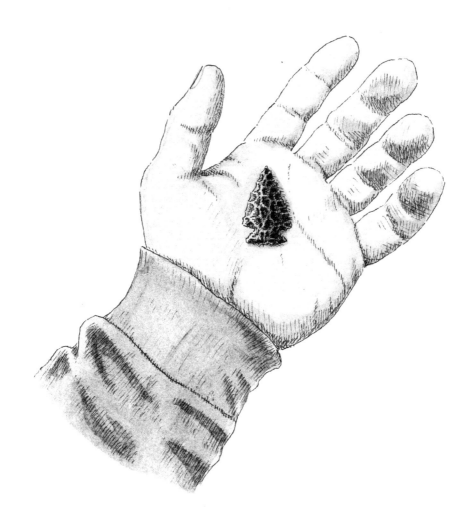

An archaeologist finds human artifacts with a scratch, scrape and sift. Soil layers reveal traces where people hunted and lived.

Botanists survey woodsy plants on the sensitive list. They guide the way to treat them right. Some need shade and some need light.

Foresters count the trees and check the size. A healthy forest is their prize. When they know which seeds to sow, they make a plan to help trees grow.

A little thinning is what this forest needs.

With a snap and wrap of the forester's tape it's harvest time in the working forest. Measure and mark the crowded and weak. Size and select for lots of board feet. The wood adds up when tallying tall trees.

A faller's chainsaw hums, cutting and bucking.
The feller-buncher grapples' tree-hugging grip
keeps the logs coming.

Lift, pull. Lift, pull. Again and again. The skidders drag and the logs roll in. With the logging truck's load racked, stacked and bound, the driver hauls the logs to town.

At the mill yard, the unloading begins.
Whip-snap of the scaler's log tape. Measure
and weigh then look for defects. A crane
hoists them high and stacks them in decks.

Saws slice, dice and transform the logs into neatly stacked lumber. The shaver peels poles from lanky, long logs.

A wood hog grinds leftover wood scraps. The finest chunky chips divert for making paper pulp. The rest goes to the fuel house. Then up the chute to the boiler. The fuelwood churns and burns, producing high-pressure steam. Whirling turbines turn out electricity that's clean.

A pole baler loads the long pole
trailer. Forklifts pack and stack the train
with racks of lumber.

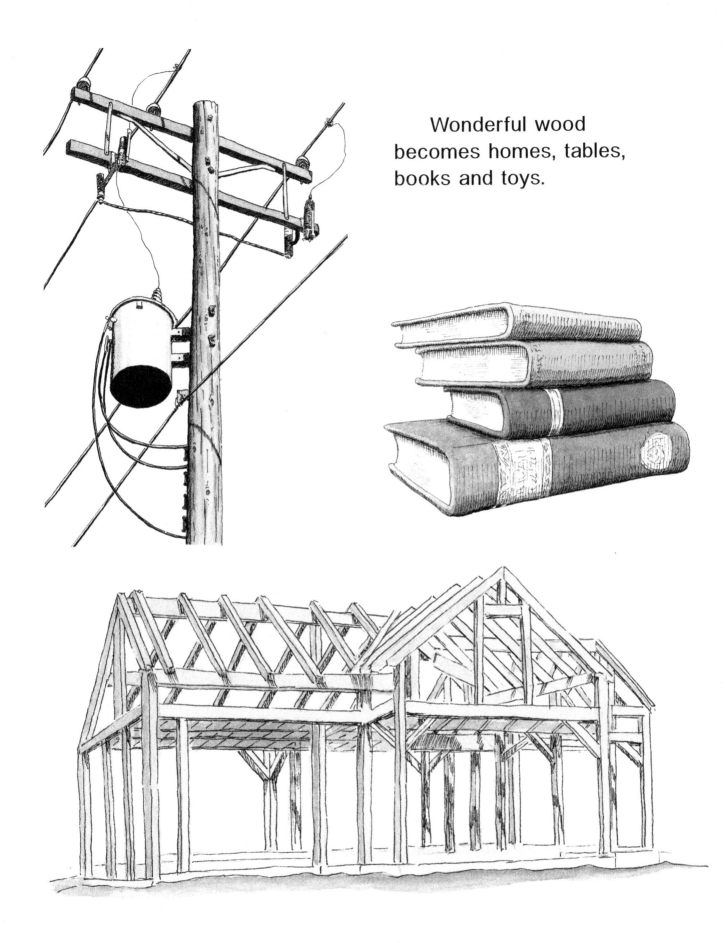

Wonderful wood
becomes homes, tables,
books and toys.

Back in the woods, it's time for the cleanup crew. A wood-chipper chews leftover tree tippy-tops. Controlled fire, nature's tidy-up tool, cleans the forest floor. Planting grass in a fresh straw bed keeps the soil from washing away.

Tree planters renew the forest. Their hoedad rhythm fills the hills.

Scalp. Break. Plant. Pack.
Scalp. Break. Plant. Pack.

Millions of trees are planted this way.

Slap-slap-slap-slap. A bear cub scampers up a tree.

Chit-a-chat. Chit-a-chat. Squirrels skedaddle up, down, across and around.

Look-at-that. Look-at-that. A child explores the working forest abuzz with activity.

Forester

Species: Human

Gender: any

Education: on the job training and/or university education especially in environmental science

Degree: Science

Licensing: typically required for writing harvest plans

Habitat: forests

Work Activities: cruising, marking, hiking, forest planning

Temperament: must be willing to work outdoors, alone or with a team, long hours in all kinds of weather

Specialties: log buying, timber harvesting, logging engineer, forest planner, research, inventory, reforestation, environmental inspector

Purpose Served to Society: maintain and improve environmental health of forest ecosystem while providing sustainable and affordable wood products

diameter tape

cruiser's vest

marking paint

Biltmore stick

logger's tape

Logger

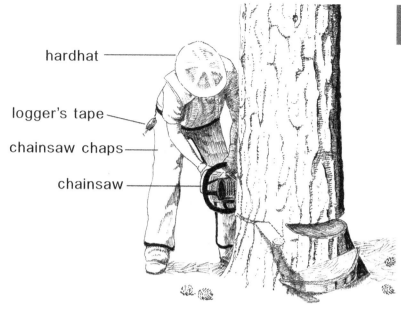

hardhat

logger's tape

chainsaw chaps

chainsaw

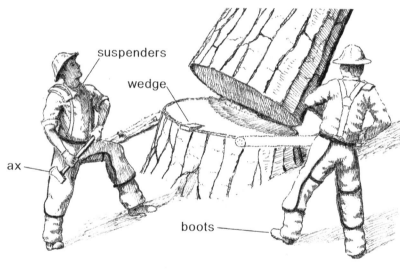

suspenders

wedge

ax

boots

Species: Human

Gender: any

Education: on the job training and must learn about environmental rules

Habitat: forests

Work Activities: hill climbing, problem solving, following the logging plan, cutting trees, bucking logs, choker setting, loading and hauling logs

Temperament: a strong mind and body, and be willing to work outdoors in bad weather

Specialties: pole logging, cable logging, helicopter logging, mechanized logging, salvage logging

Purpose Served to Society: provide sustainable and affordable wood products

Red Tail Publishing
Established 1993

P.O. Box 1477, Anderson, CA 96007
www.redtail.com

TIMBER!

Hardback ISBN13: 978-1-941950-05-0   Paperback ISBN13: 978-1-941950-06-7   Also available as ebook.

facebook.com/TimberPictureBook   facebook.com/RedTailPublishing

CPSIA information can be obtained
at www.ICGtesting.com
Printed in the USA
BVOW05s0923230117
474099BV00001B/1/P